10 THINGS
I WISH I'D KNOWN
ABOUT SELF-PUBLISHING

10 THINGS
I WISH I'D KNOWN
ABOUT SELF-PUBLISHING

Goose Your Muse Tips for Creatives Series

Yvonne Kohano

Nanokas Press
A Division of Kochanowski Enterprises
Copyright © 2017

10 THINGS I WISH I'D KNOWN ABOUT SELF-PUBLISHING
Goose Your Muse Tips for Creatives Series
Copyright © 2017 by Y J Kohano

Nanokas Press/KE Press books may be ordered through booksellers or by contacting:

Kochanowski Enterprises/Nanokas Press
PO Box 1274
Clackamas, OR 97015-9594
www.yvonnekohano.com
yvonne@yvonnekohano.com

Cover design: John Kochanowski

ISBN:
978-1-940738-60-4 (e)
978-1-940738-59-8 (sc)

Nanokas Press First Edition: 10-09-2017

Contents

WHY I WROTE THIS BOOK.. 1

MY STORY AND I'M STICKING TO IT............................. 4

1 – WRITE NEW WORDS FAST 8

What Writing Fast Means... 9

How I Do It... 11

Avoiding the Research Rabbit Hole 12

Spelling, Grammar and Punctuation 15

Plot Shifts 16

Out of Ideas – Not 17

If Writing Fast is Impossible 19

2 – EDIT SLOW.. 21

The Voice in Your Head.. 22

Point of View Pitfalls 24

Multiple Passes 26

More Pets to Play With 30

Synonyms and Vibrancy 31

Editing Roundup 33

3 – DECIDE ON BRANDS AND STANDARDS 34

Format and Layout... 35

Interior Standards 37

Your Social Footprints 41

Consistent Themes and Styles 44

In Charge of YOU 45

4 – PREPARE YOUR BOOK FOR RELEASE................... 47

Trustworthy People.. 48

Paying People 50

Learning New Skills 52

Your Three-Legged Stool... 54

5 – OWN YOUR ISBNs 56

Following the Money, Part One...................................... 57

How Many ISBNs 59

Barcodes 60

Copyright... 61

Keeping Your Control 63

6 – DEMAND ACCOUNTABILITY.................................. 64

Following the Money, Part Two...................................... 64

Get It in Writing... 68

Who Else Do I Need? 69
I Can't Afford This! 71
7 – DOCUMENT YOUR METADATA **72**
Metadata Recordkeeping 73
Numbers in One Place 75
Leaving a Trail 77
8 – AVOID TECHNOLOGY DISTRACTIONS **78**
WORD COUNT COMES FIRST 79
One Place You Shouldn't Scrimp 81
Social Media, Blogging and Other Hubbub 83
Learn Your Audience 85
Email List Control 87
Technology as a Tool 90
9 – PROMOTE THYSELF **92**
Promotion = Our Responsibility 93
Easy Outreach 94
Trained Extrovert Made Simple 95
Cue the Business Cards 100
DON'T Do This If You're Not 'On' 102
Little Bites, Little Wins 103
10 – BUILD YOUR WRITING TRIBE **104**
Networking Breeds Success 104
How I Built My Tribe 105
Introverts Hate Conferences 108
Writing Community Nonwriters 111
THE FINAL RULE **112**
Also by Yvonne Kohano **115**
About the Author **117**

10 THINGS
I WISH I'D KNOWN
ABOUT SELF-PUBLISHING

WHY I WROTE THIS BOOK

It KILLS me to know writers, dedicated and excited and just a little scared, stumble when it comes time to self-publish their book. I hate seeing them weighted down by honest mistakes they could have avoided, if only they knew who to ask. I'd love to help each of them find the WAY without the hassle and pain.

I began releasing my fiction books in a time that seems like the dark ages now, and yet, it was only a shade over five years ago. Some things have gotten better and become easier. Other things, sadly, remain a challenge.

> *Learn enough here to decide where you spend*
> *your time and money next.*

I've taken what I know to be true, from my own experiences and those of friends and close acquaintances, plus lessons taught in countless workshops, and put them into these ten considerations for anyone considering self-publishing. Many of these apply to traditional publishing too, so listen up if you're heading down that road.

I know this isn't everything people need to know at a level of detail that answers all the questions. Each topic could be its own book, and maybe I'll write those someday. For now, I want to evangelize on what I think it is important for you to consider as you prepare your wonderful story, memoir or self-help account for blast-off into the big world of readership.

To avoid misunderstandings, this is not EVERYTHING you need to know about self-publishing, but it is enough to have you thinking about where to take your next deep dive and invest time and money. Much of what I refer to in specific examples focuses on fiction writing. The rules apply to more than the storytelling world, however. Take away what you need and apply it as it best fits your writing environment.

In this book, I've provided tips on how to bypass road blocks to your success, speed toward completion of your journey, and relax at a peaceful rest area when each phase is completed. There are a few givens in here, and in other places,

I outline your options. When you come to a fork in the road, it's always good to know what lies ahead along each path.

What I know, I know from experience. The brutal, costly, painful kind. Don't make my mistakes. Avoid the accidents and detours, and you'll have yourself a pleasant, enriching indie journey.

Let's take this trip together!

MY STORY AND I'M STICKING TO IT

I didn't know what I didn't know, despite hours, days, weeks of researching. I have more folders of workshop materials than I want to count. I could have taken a very nice vacation – or three – on the money I spent to learn things – and still, I didn't know. No one told me, I think because they didn't know either. We were all paddling along, hoping to figure it out before we went over Niagara Falls heading to the rocks below without the benefit of a barrel to protect us.

First, a little background about me. I have multiple college degrees, the kind that made me spend a significant portion of my years in research and practice and analysis and implementation. I ran a successful consulting company long enough to make my hair turn gray. I had nonfiction publications to my name, the traditional kind. My writing skills as a storyteller were established, because that's what management consultants and university professors do – we tell stories to help others understand difficult topics and make change happen.

And still, I didn't know.

QUALITY <-> CONTROL <-> READERS

In 2011, self-publishing was changing at such a rapid pace, it made our hair fly behind us like a billowing curtain. Short hairs, too! If you thought you'd mastered the conversion system of one distributor or understood the array of services an organization provided, your knowledge was out of date before the next moon rise. Attend a workshop at a conference, and by the time you flew home, you needed a refresher on recent modifications and revisions.

Thankfully, things have slowed to a less hectic pace, though shifts are still dramatic and dynamic. We call ourselves 'indies' now, and the only people who still poo-poo self-publishing do so at the risk of being ostracized and laughed at. Leap-frogging successes happen every day, in terms of trying new techniques to reach the most important people in our world, our readers. Technology trips us up as well as saves us. Workshops galore distract us.

Laws change. Players change. Systems change. Yet certain rules of the self-publishing road remain constant. Here are the three biggies:

WORD QUALITY. You need it.

PUBLISHING CONTROL. You want it.

DEDICATED READERS. You must have them.

(And you need the first two to get them!)

Word quality is vital to be a successful indie – and even that isn't a guarantee of success. You need to implement every tool in your writing craft toolbox, without skipping steps and hoping for the best. The reason self-publishing received such a bad rap for years was because it struggled under the perception that people unable to 'make it' in the traditional publishing arena due to poor quality flooded its ranks, and that was too often true. Thankfully, now you can't afford to put junk out there, because your competition is handing out gold.

What do I mean by control? The closer you are to calling the shots at each stage of your indie system, the better. This does not mean you need to do it all yourself – most of us can't, not sustainably. Your role as the puppeteer pulling the strings means you don't allow Pinocchio to dance on his own.

Readership, avid fans who devour everything we put out, is what we all aspire to. After all, if you're not in this to make the cha-ching, why did you buy this book? If your hope is to release a memoir you present only to family and a few close friends, stop reading now. You won't need this, because they won't care. They'll buy your book anyway because they love you. If you want to make money as an author, please carry on.

Diving into the lessons, you're going to be frightened, disappointed, and dismayed. Get over it. You're a writer, and you want to be an author, and you CAN be a successful one. Each time you ignore these words to the wise and say they can't possibly apply to you, you put yourself a further distance from success as an indie. Pull up your big girl panties or your big boy boxers. You're a self-publishing professional. You can do this!

1 – WRITE NEW WORDS FAST

I remember the good old days, when my focus was on new words and the characters yacking in my head and the way the plot evolved. That was ALL I cared about. If I used passive tense more than active or head-hopped or included flawed motivations, I didn't know it. All I knew was that I was writing a story and I loved it.

Fast forward a few years. I've been through editing grinds, my own and with paid professionals. I learned more about craft intricacies than I thought existed. (I truly think there are more craft 'rules' today than ever before in the literary world, simply because we have access to more people's opinions. Topic for another book.) I suffered through discordant advice, confusion to the point of tears, and frustrations from changing winds of opinion about what was 'right'.

In that turbulent time, I forgot how to write fast. I've since remembered, and many writers ask me how I do it. Here's the skinny.

What Writing Fast Means

Does the rapid fire click of my nails on the keyboard make you sweat? You and me, WRITER, in a write-off, the kind where the person with the most words at the end of the time wins.

How will you fare? Are you the kind of writer who thinks over each word selection as you're working on your first draft? Do you feel COMPELLED to research the era-specific term or the correct make and model of car or the distance between two points the characters are traversing NOW?

You will not be able to write fast, because you will be distracted by the minutiae. I'll be taking home the chocolate bar and the bottle of wine at the end of the hour.

Don't get caught up in details and decisions

you can easily fill in later.

That will slow you down!

On the other hand, if you develop your system of making inline notes, providing cues and reminders for later in-depth analysis, we might be battling a bit. And if you can turn off your inner editor? We'll be duking it out, my friend, and I might be the one sweating!

It doesn't matter if you're a plotter (the kind of writer who outlines a book before they begin writing it) or a pantser (no outline, just flowing with it) or somewhere in between. We can ALL become caught up in the details and want to fix them. Right. NOW. It slows us down.

Our inner editor also screams at us. "No, not that word. It isn't right. You need to find the correct word. You can't move forward without the perfect active verb."

Lock the inner editor in a closet until it's time to edit. Yes, you do need that level of exquisite excellence, *but not now*. Be messy. Let it go. Come back to these changes later. I promise, that editor will be around and ready to help you then. *But not now*. NOW, you need to capture the ideas and nuances as best you can, and save the fine-tuning for later.

How I Do It

When I'm in the groove and writing fast, I don't worry about using the same descriptive word three times in the same paragraph. I don't quibble about excessive character tags. I even ignore passive tense, for the most part (though I find that as I continue down my own road, I'm writing active tense as part of my natural flow).

About the only thing I worry about is head-hopping. That's where a writer expresses the story from one character's point of view (perspective) and then, mid-paragraph or section or chapter, without warning the poor *confused* reader, switches to another character's head. Ergo, head-hopping. I think it bugs me so much that I find if I'm doing it, it slams on my mental brakes faster than a tailgater in a rush hour traffic jam. For me, fixing it later takes more time than I want to spend, so I try to avoid it in the first place.

Ignore the imperfections. That's why it's called a first draft. You'll revise, edit, weep with joy, declare it the best thing ever – and then say it's the worst piece possibly written and want to shred any paper copies and slam a hammer on the digital drive. You won't. You'll release it anyway. That's part of the process.

When I come to a place in my first draft where a character wants to sip a unique brand of Scotch, or she rides a special model of Harley, I make an ALL CAPS note to research it. That's it. I keep typing.

If the word choice isn't coming to me, I keep going. I have an editing pass for that. Ditto on active tense. I check character inconsistencies in a special editing pass too. I save all of that – ALL OF IT – for editing. I keep writing as fast as I can, because I don't want any plot or scheme to disappear because I dallied too long on a synonym.

Avoiding the Research Rabbit Hole

I am betting you've been there. You think, "This will just take a second." You open your browser and add in the search term, and up pop a dozen or more top entries for your digging pleasure. I've done this too! I looked up that brand of Scotch, which led me to their intriguing website, which led me to a listing of B&Bs in the area. Before I knew it, I scrolled through tour possibilities even though I have NO PLAN to visit this country far away and taste the Scotch in person. *An hour later, I crawled out of the rabbit hole, shaking my head, blinking at the sunlight and wondering what happened.*

Now, as I type about the character lifting the bottle of SCOTCH and offering it to his friend, who makes a pithy comment about the guy's taste in SCOTCH. It's easy to scan visually for all-caps, leaving that research activity for some time when I've written my new words for the day and my brain is otherwise unavailable for creation. But loitering in the research zone? Oh yes!

Another way to mark these sections and make them automatically searchable is a series of symbols. Something like %%% or &&& or ??? marks research to be done or a missing thought or transition. When you are ready to edit for those kinds of issues, you plug your symbols series into the search function of your word processor and click them off, one by one.

You might be wondering why I don't use colored highlighting or a comments bubble to mark areas that need work. In Microsoft Word, my writing software of choice, some of those command functions leave behind code you cannot see in your document after you accept a change or delete the original text. The trail allows you to return to a previous version (pre-comment-acceptance), so something must be there to mark it. Other software programs have similar features that also leave trails of code behind.

> **ALL CAPS is an effective way to mark areas you know need work.**

Back in the day three or four years ago, early conversion programs took your document and turned each electronic byte into a flowable format readable by ereaders. Codes turned into gibberish on the ereader screen. This was a very common problem requiring significant time to fix in your proof files. There were workarounds, but those also took precious time.

Buried coding doesn't seem as prevalent an issue today, but I've still seen it happening with formatting, punctuation and some wording, so I avoid it. Experiment if you like and see if you can break the systems. I'd rather spend my time setting it up to NOT happen than fixing it later. Tedious!

Spelling, Grammar and Punctuation

You know that function, where Word (or your software of choice) underlines a word to let you know you goofed in its spelling or usage? It can seem like it's blinking in neon, shouting at you, with large arrows flashing and screaming your name. Some writer friends swear the sight of a misspelled word drives them crazy.

Turn off that function if it makes you nuts. Run your spelling and grammatical checks at the end of your writing day. Doing it in-line (like the middle of a sentence) with your original creations will only slow you down. That backspace key is NOT your best friend!

What about those missing commas or periods, you might ask? Ignore those too. I've heard people worry they'll miss them later, when they work on the editing pass(es) where they focus on such things. I doubt you will, if you're careful and edit slow. I read my text in my head, pretending I'm reading an audio book. Some people read it out loud. You WILL catch them!

Plot Shifts

You might be curious about what I, as a pantser, do when the characters frolic off in a new direction, one that doesn't exactly jive with their path before. I don't panic. My characters are always an unruly bunch and they do what they want, when they want, and how they want. I can't control them, only channel what they tell me. Often, they lead me in a direction I hadn't considered. If we've taken a wrong turn, I find I recognize it quickly. You'll know the feeling. The woods grow dark. Tree branches scratch your cheeks and snag your clothes. A malevolent presence seems to be watching you, raising the hairs on the back of your neck. That sort of thing.

Plot shifts happen, even to plotters who outline to a level of angst I cannot imagine. I might find that the action happening NOW requires set-up in a previous chapter. Or I need to add a feature or characteristic to my heroine. Or a sinister something happens to my hero that I should foreshadow at a point long before the one I'm at now.

I've used two techniques here. I use the ALL CAPS method to note what I need to add in a scene that comes before. I might even note to myself where I think this should go. I don't worry about placing it there now. That slows me down.

The other method I've used is a blank page at the beginning of my manuscript (MS). (It never stays blank for long.) I quickly toggle to that page and make a note of what I must explain, set up, or foreshadow. Then I zoom back to the new words and keep going. Going to the beginning and then to the spot of new words takes time and additional keystrokes, so it's slower, but sometimes if there's a lot to say, it's tidier.

Out of Ideas – Not

I hear this from writers as a painful refrain, a wail screeched into the unknown. "What if I write so fast, I run out of ideas?"

Relax! You will <u>always</u> have ideas. Sometimes it just takes longer to tap into them than others. Writing fast, writing until you've written everything you know at that session, doesn't mean there is nothing left to say. Triggers will help you find the next words.

I have two tricks to tame the no-ideas fears:

I stop in the middle of a paragraph or a sentence. I know what's to come next, which gets me started for my next writing session.

If I think I have nothing to say, staring blankly at the blinking cursor, I write something – anything – else. Gibberish, even. I just start writing. It comes to me.

There are many other tricks. Keep an idea file. Go to the notes you have for your work in progress and tackle one of those. Write scenes out of order. Rewrite a scene you aren't happy with, changing the character point of view. Turn a comedy into a tragedy, and a horror story into a farce. Add humor. Subtract it. The list is truly endless. CHANGE

SOMETHING. That is often enough to get you going, and you'll be galloping along on the word count before you know it.

And if *none of that* works, examine why. Sit quietly, or take a walk. Concentrate on the wonder of being able to write something other people will read. Tell yourself about all the reasons you love being a writer. Just the good stuff.

Then put fingers to keyboard or pen to paper and WRITE!

If Writing Fast is Impossible

You might have noticed that I never said HOW fast is *FAST.* That's because it's different for each of us. A dear friend with whom I share a writing tribe feels like she's approached the speed of sound when she writes two thousand words a week. That, for me, is an hourly count. Different people, different keystrokes. **There is no one ONLY way.**

The point is to write as fast as YOU can. I hear many writers complain that they hate editing, and I think it's because they want to move on to the next great idea they already had. Write as fast as you can anyway, because it's much, much easier to revise words on a page than it is to stare at a blank one!

2 – EDIT SLOW

How slow is slow editing?

The answer is: as slow as it needs to be. This is an area where I see many writers rushing to an unsatisfactory finish, and not applying the care and attention required to turn out their best work. Note that I said 'their' best work, not the best piece of genre fiction, literary fiction nonfiction self-help or memoir every written. We can all only do as much as we're capable of. Make a commitment to deliberate editing, and the quality of your work becomes better with time and effort.

> *Deliberate editing done slowly and with care improves your future rough drafts along with your current work.*

If you've followed the fast writing effort, your first draft is messy and has *needs*. Here are some major editing categories writers could focus on with better results to address them. (This is BEFORE you hire an editor, mind you.)

The Voice in Your Head

Passive voice creates its own set of roadblocks to reader enjoyment of your work. It slows down the reader's progress. It is most often a sign of the dreaded *telling*, not *showing*. Here's an example.

The enemy was defeated by the battalion.

The subject – the enemy – wasn't the do-er. The battalion did the deed. The subject passively lays around, stomped upon.

In active tense, where you are showing instead of telling, this would be:

The battalion defeated the enemy.

Read the two sentences aloud, and focus on the images suggested by each one. From the second example, I visualize the battalion charging up the hill, shouts of rage and fury flying from their lips, as they swamp the enemy and overrun them. That's what we want. Let the reader paint the picture in their own mind about the scene. They're smart, and they love to participate in the story in this way! If you tell them too much, you'll bore them.

There *are* times we use passive tense to slow action and let the reader catch their breath, or to sneak up on a reader before a big splash of action. Mixing up sentence structures can also lead us to select a passive voice. These pacing and style decisions arise from our <u>deliberate</u> choice in one of our many fine-tuning editorial passes. Beware of too much passivity, because like too much telling, it disappoints rather than gratifies your readers.

If you study active versus passive tense in detail – and I encourage you to do just that – you'll find active becomes your natural go-to voice when you write fast. If you spend an inordinate amount of time editing and revising a manuscript of great length to turn passive into active, you'll learn your lesson.

Believe me, it becomes easier with practice. (I even find myself *talking* in active voice now!)

Point of View Pitfalls

Point of view (POV) refers to the lens through which the reader sees the action happening. I mentioned head-hopping before, when that POV shifts in the middle of a section, or paragraph, or thought. Why should you care if this happens in YOUR book?

Head-hopping from one POV to another in a place that doesn't make sense *pulls the reader out of your story*. They read a passage, then re-read it, and suddenly they're confused and looking around for the answer and distracted because something else – some bright shiny thing that *IS NOT* your story suddenly makes more sense to them.

The other major POV pitfall is showing something happening from the perspective of someone *who cannot know or see it*. Unless he or she can read minds, the character doesn't know what the other person is thinking or feeling. They can make assumptions, but they won't know for sure. (A tip –

This would be a great point in your story to add actions – showing, not telling – that gives the readers clues about whether those assumptions are right or wrong. A character squirming or giggling are great examples of this.)

Sadly, I've seen poorly edited work, even traditionally published pieces, glossing over sloppy POV shifts that bring a reader up short. Do not be that author. Be the one who shows the reader that indies work harder to earn their reading time by treating POV with loving care.

How do I manage POV? If I think a passage is sloppy, I take it apart, sentence by sentence, and analyze who *knows* what and who can *say* what. Yes, it can be tedious. I had a 90,000-word novel that needed to be torn apart into little pieces and taped back together because I screwed up on POV. SO. MANY. TIMES. I learned my lesson the hard way!

Remember…

Only POV characters reveal feelings or emotions.

Any thoughts of characters outside of POV will

be described by POV characters making

assumptions about them.

Each scene or chapter should have only one

POV to avoid confusing the reader.

Changing POVs should be clearly

indicated with a break, and the fewer in a

chapter, the better.

There are many great courses, workshops and guides to help you learn successful POV. The best way to master it, though, is to write a lot. Write scenes you may never use, just to practice. Write a scene from one character's POV, then turn around and write it only from the other's. You will learn so much (and avoid a total, mind-numbing rewrite in the process) when you become overly conscious of POV shifts.

Multiple Passes

I find I best handle editing with multiple passes, each with a specific purpose. Some revision passes scream for completion as soon as I type THE END on the manuscript. Others are best left to a time when I've had distance from the work and can see it more clearly.

Here's an example of the purposes of my editing passes:

Open research items.

Anything on my list at the beginning of the document. In this case, I might only make an ALL CAPS note in-line and come back to it later, or I might take the time necessary to make the full change now. It depends on how much I should revise.

Anything in-line in ALL CAPS that I haven't yet modified.

Plot inconsistencies or areas where I strayed and need to return to the main point of a scene.

A first pass at word choices, focusing on multiple uses of the same word.

A first pass at changing tense from passive to active.

That's my first set of editing passes. Then, I step away from the manuscript and let the pot bubble for a while. (Good stew takes time to make!) How long depends on my plans for the timing of a release. The minimum I've found working best for me is a month for a full-length novel, and a week for a short novella or self-help book. You'll know what's good for you. Give yourself permission to step away for a while, and you'll see the great stuff and the necessary revisions more clearly.

When I pick up the manuscript again, I begin with a scan of the whole document without the intention of making changes. This refreshes me on the characters, motivations, and plot and conflict. The same holds true for nonfiction, like this book, and any other kind of writing.

The scan tells me where I should focus my attentions first. Generally, these fall in the following categories (in no implied order):

Tense (change passive to active)

Characters not operating according to their true

motivations

Characters who could be in greater conflict

Making the worst that could happen, happen

Addition of all five senses in character

experiences

Setting and location issues

Plot inconsistencies

Snooze-worthy dialogue

Too many dialogue tags

Colloquialisms and styles in dialogue

I'm careful when it comes to dialogue. People don't talk like a style manual. Make that part real, reflective of how those folks would talk, and make it consistent for that character throughout your story.

More Pets to Play With

The lists of pet words are almost as numerous as the words themselves. Here are a few I have not yet mentioned (mostly because my poor fingers shake when I use them!)

Pet words (just, that, should, thought, wondered)

And or But at the beginning of a sentence

Now and Then to show action

Indirect phrases of passivity (there is, there are)

Verbs ending in -ing

Adverbs ending in -ly

Repetitive words in a paragraph or scene

Repetitive words beginning consecutive

paragraphs

Repetitive sentence construction

Repetitive paragraph construction

And the list goes on. Can you decide to use repetition, adverbs or any pet words? Of course, but it should be choice, not rushing sloppiness, that drives you.

Using your search engine to find advice on pet words, crutch words, and common editing problems is only one step in your process. The more important action occurs when you identify YOUR pet problems and implement an editing pass to catch those issues – before your manuscript goes to an editor.

Synonyms and Vibrancy

One final editing pass that bears mention is the one where your ho-hum language morphs into vibrant literacy. The use of powerful words takes your writing to the next level. What do you see in your mind's eye when you read stumbled instead of ran? Or enraged instead of mad? Find a new word that better describes the feelings, emotions and 'show' of what's happening through the magic of synonyms.

I use three different methods to identify alternative words. Microsoft Word includes a synonym finder, and that's usually my first recourse. A quick right-click on the word, and a list of choices and their uses appears on my screen alongside my text.

On a more sophisticated level, MasterWriter, a cloud-based solution, lists synonyms, antonyms (opposites), definitions, and use in phrases. I pay the annual fee gladly, because this has been the most complete guide I've found that's also easy and quick to use. I leave the program open in my browser, click over to it when I need choices, and type in the word. Boom!

At another level that nonetheless can be as effective, buy yourself a good (by that, I mean more than pocket-sized) thesaurus in book form. Yes, your fingers will need to do the walking, but browsing through it might also suggest other words you can replace to increase the intensity of your drama and humor. Say it better with synonyms!

> **Editing – good editing – is an iterative and repetitive process.**

Editing Roundup

Many solid craft resources on what to edit and when are available on the market. Study them with your writing alongside. Make a checklist of the common problems your writing faces, and use that to guide your editing passes.

P A S S E S. Don't scrimp on this level of attention! Editing takes more than a handful of passes. Trying to do too much in one sweep means you'll miss things – and kick yourself later. And don't forget to use a non-YOU editor!

3 – DECIDE ON BRANDS AND STANDARDS

Brand is typically thought of as a marketing term, an identity in the market. It is that, and it is so much more. It pays for you to make brand decisions now, to avoid confusing or disappointing your eventual reading audience.

I think of brand at three levels when applied to our writing life:

> *Brand is the design of what we do, the formats for our books and newsletters and anything else we produce.*
>
> *Brand is the image we project through our public expressions, our book covers representing us, our social trails, and our sites.*

Brand is the writing style we become known for,

the proposition our readers expect from

our work.

Each of these areas warrants our early consideration to avoid a load of rework later.

Format and Layout

I thought I understood it, but I was four books in before I had a clue. It took me two more titles to "get it". Then it took a long, long time to make the changes necessary to align everything.

I was so excited to release those first few books. Back in the day of "The Pure Joy of Writing", as I call it, I had a vision for how I thought I wanted my books to look. I'd taken the brand marketing courses and conference workshops. A background of a pine tree would grace each cover. The photo inserted under the title would represent something thematic in the story. The blurb would hint at the mysterious conflict.

Wrong! Book One came out, and I liked the layout of the cover, but it didn't pop as a thumbnail – too busy. Book Two had a different problem, with the same pine background making it indiscernible from the first book at a quick glance. Readers were already confused!

Plus, the blurbs didn't pop either. While I worked with an editor and used their suggestions, they too missed the boat because they weren't familiar enough with my work. I missed the whole ocean!

> ***Learn what professional looks like so you can emulate it.***

I learned quite a few things about formatting and style in those first books. I worked with professional designers for the interiors, and they taught me about layout standards for new chapters, margins, and spacing. How would the interior of my books look? They were all part of a series, so giving them the same appearance was important.

Later in the series, I realized my vision for the covers wasn't going to be the best one to communicate the stories. I had to give it up. You might need to as well. Better yet, set yourself up early on for a successful brand concept by bouncing options off potential readers.

Cover design and interior design are two parts of the self-publishing process where learning from professionals is a great way to spend your money wisely. Your cover needs to pop when it's a thumbnail on a search engine or when it's on paper. You don't want to suffer from run-ons when you really intended to use a scene break in your ebook. You want your books to look professional. Learn what that looks like, and then decide if doing it yourself will work for you.

Interior Standards

I'm beginning here because it might be the easiest sector of brand to tackle. Interior standards refer to how you set up the formatting of your book inside – and it's more than that. This refers to both ebooks and paper versions – and each can be different.

When you hire a professional book formatter, they will take care of the 'look' inside your books. You certainly have a say in the matter, however. How do you decide what the insides should look like?

> **Format with your readers' comfort in mind.**

First and foremost, have your readers' comfort in mind when you format your book. That means keeping the design easy to read. Conform to what's generally accepted in your genre. Be yourself, but not too different, because that can make it harder for readers to engage with your books.

Developing your 'look' is a simple process. Explore your market first. That means looking inside the books in your genre. I visit a physical book store and seek out books in my genre. I flip through titles that I aspire to be (okay, I'll admit I look at the bestsellers) and see how they have their sections laid out. I check:

Sections included as front matter (things in the

front of the book that are not your original

writing)

How the title page is laid out

What chapter headings look like

What's indented, and what isn't (like the first

paragraph of a new chapter)

Design for section breaks (like a little logo)

Type font used

Spacing between paragraphs

Headers or footers

Back matter

Pick apart the books you choose to review like you're a detective and the clue to solve the case is hidden in these pages. It is! Even a simple thing like the width of the margins is important.

"Margins, really?" Yes, really. On one of my early paperback versions, I tried to 'save' on the cost of production by narrowing the margins. As a result, text ran close to the spine on each page, making it harder for people to read. When a reader is frustrated by *ANY* part of the reading experience, they are more likely to set the book aside in favor of something that's not fighting them.

For ebooks, you'll be doing the same thing, though your decisions will be different. Ebooks are "flowable", meaning you aren't worried about headers or page numbers. Text size can be changed in most ereader software, giving the user-reader control of that aspect of the reading experience. If, for example, you leave a large space between the chapter number and the beginning of text, that might mean the chapter heading is on its own page. That might not be the experience you want to offer.

Ebook trends also come into consideration in your formatting. You'll be doing the same kinds of things to 'shop the competition'. I have an ereader, and I regularly read in my genres. I look at what the big sellers are doing for their interiors. Trends shift. For example, in a paper book, the copyright page is usually placed in the front matter. In ebooks, a few hardy souls began putting it in back. They sold a lot of books and now many ebooks have the copyright page in back. Why? Because readers don't usually read that, so why delay getting them into the story by putting it in front?

Don't have an ereader or like ebooks, period? Your readers <u>do</u>, so you still need to shop around. You can visit the major book buying sites and use the 'look inside' function most of them have these days. Check out what others are doing on interior formats in that way, if you can't examine them on an ereading platform yourself.

Feeling overwhelmed? Don't be! This is your business, and like any business, you need design ideas to determine the direction you feel comfortable going, *even when you hire someone else to execute it*. You're going for a 'look' that represents you and what you are selling. Select one small step, take it, then place your foot for the next one.

Your Social Footprints

Your books are only one aspect of the outer 'you' people see. Another brand concept embraces the other appearances you expose to your readers, like a website, blog, newsletter, and social media.

You don't need any of these things to launch a book. You can even forget about them with a series. However, if you want to grow your reader base, you must make it easy for them to find you, and that's often accomplished by being visible where they live and play.

> **Social media presence isn't a requirement to launch your book, but it helps readers find you and fall in love with your work.**

I'll return for a moment to my pine tree background, because it lived on in infamy for longer than it should have. I used that background as the header on my webpage. I used it on my business cards. It appeared on my newsletters and braced the headers of my social media profiles. It covered the six-foot banner I hung at face to face events. Until I became ruthless and chopped that pine tree down, it grew everywhere.

With the right image, this kind of blanketing is a powerful thing. But what if you want to change it? What if it doesn't represent your work well? Your image falls to the bottom of the buy list with a dull thud, never to be heard from again.

Think carefully about the image you want to project to your potential audience. I'll harp on this again – what is the competition doing? Visit their websites. Subscribe to their blogs, if they have them. Get their newsletters. Play in their sandbox, even if you don't want it to be yours.

It's not just how images look, but how you sound that's important. Some authors take a political stand. Others focus on the world they create. Some who write in a specific style, like historical, might also write their newsletters in the same colloquial style. Others might pick a topic that interests them, as I do with travel and gardening and cooking, and make that a regular component of their reader outreach.

There is no one RIGHT way – there's just the RIGHT way for *you*. You're building reader expectations. They grow comfortable with those, and your writing style, and through that, you. That's what you want. They'll then follow YOU, even when you might stray a bit on your path.

Consistent Themes and Styles

I like to write a series. I like the comfort I receive from knowing the location and repeating characters. Readers like that too. Part of that is the series theme I create, one they enjoy and resonates with them, encouraging them to come back for more. The other part is the style I use, the voice they're used to hearing from my work.

But what is theme? You don't need to write in a series format to have one. The theme is something readers come to know you for. I write about self-acceptance as a path to love – a lot. I write about facing down your worst fears and not just surviving but triumphing – a lot. My primary characters go through these things – and the reader knows they'll always find a satisfactory resolution to the problems blocking their path. They read to find out HOW they make it across that transition zone.

THEME = thumbnail of conflict and

resolution

STYLE = how you write about it

Style is how you write. In Flynn's Crossing, I have two primary characters in each book. I write them in third person deep point of view – always. (That's the topic for a book by itself too.) In a new series I'm working on, the characters are written in first person, and will be throughout. Consistency makes readers comfortable.

What happens if you discover your theme or style isn't RIGHT? It doesn't fit, or it isn't what you thought it was, or you're no longer comfortable with it. That's okay. Make the change that works best for the story. If it works, go back and adjust what came before. It could be as simple as rewriting book blurbs to focus attention on a different aspect. Only rework the past, though, if it doesn't hold you back from moving forward.

In Charge of YOU

I covered a lot in this section, and your head is probably spinning. That's normal. Remember, you might be hiring out many of these tasks. Hire the right people, and they will help you formulate these standards for your work. You're still the CEO of your authorship, and you guide them with your ideas and your enthusiasm.

4 – PREPARE YOUR BOOK FOR RELEASE

Most of us are not ready to take on the complete list of tasks in the self-publishing world from the beginning of our indie career. Many people are afraid of going indie because of the many required tasks. Don't be. There are guides to follow. You will grow. You didn't learn to tie your shoes or ride a bike or read words overnight. This is no different, and you can learn these skills too.

My advice is – *do as much to prepare your book for release yourself as you can, based on your skills, time and money.* Some activities need a second set of eyes, like editing and proofreading, but others such as formatting can be learned, eliminating a middle person. That leaves more money in your pocket, meaning you can spend more on editing and advertising.

This all comes back to that magic word, CONTROL. The closer you can hold things, the more flexibility you have to make changes when necessary. It's a trade-off between three specific factors:

> **Money** – *to pay someone to do each of the tasks*
>
> **Time** – *to do things yourself*
>
> **Skills** – *to perform the tasks yourself*

Weigh each of these factors carefully, and decide what path works best FOR YOU.

Trustworthy People

I spoke earlier of learning the hard way that all companies providing services are not good people. Maybe I shouldn't say people, specifically, because those companies have hardworking folks like you and me. However, the corporate structure they work under might not have your best interests in mind.

I recommend paying people to do the self-publishing work for you when:

You're only doing one book.

You don't care about learning.

You'd rather be creating, and you don't have much time.

You're starting out, to build your skills.

The first point is obvious. If you're only going to write one book, pay someone else to do the tasks you'd otherwise have to invest time and effort to learn. Unless you're crazy about doing it all yourself, and learning things you probably will never use again, it's a waste of your time.

Some people have no interest in the mechanics of getting a book to market. Or taking those technology-based steps terrifies them. Making the numerous decisions overwhelms them. That's okay. That's why author services companies stay in business, because people need them.

On the other end of the spectrum, though, are those of us who want to know how to do it – but don't know how _now_. How do we advance from novice to pro?

Paying People

You want mentors, trusted partners who help you learn. When I was a management consultant, I made it a point to help each client learn steps in the process I was performing for them. I wanted them to know more, so that next time they needed me, they could do the first few tasks themselves, if they chose to. It's the same with finding a good indie development partner.

I'll begin with who you should avoid. Stay away from companies that charge you a lot but keep all the control – artistic, design, ISBN (more on that later). If you want to change *anything* in the future, you pay the full package price again.

> **Just because it comes with the package**
>
> **doesn't mean you need it**
>
> **– or should pay for it.**

Take a close look at what comes with the package. Do you need those services and resulting products? Can you carve out what you need and jettison the rest? Will they negotiate the package price with you?

Good services providers make this about <u>you as the author</u> and <u>your written work</u>. Some might negotiate with you to decide which of their services best fit your product, then give you a package price based on your needs (not only what they're willing to put together). If they also offer the ability to select services individually, like changing a book cover later, all the better.

Your other pay-people option is putting together your own array of services. Buy the cover design from one company, and the interior formatting from another. Editing services and proofreading may not come from the same provider. If you are good at planning and synchronizing, and you have a list of good resources with people you trust, this may be the route for you. As a bonus, when you want to change a single thing, it's a lot easier to do.

You'll probably notice I didn't mention conversion and uploading in the services above. That is sometimes offered by a formatter, or people who specialize in doing only that. You can also upload your books yourself, directly with the distribution channel. As you can probably guess, direct is my choice because – wait for it – CONTROL. If I want to update the book with the latest list of all my titles, it's an easy thing to do. And yes, most distribution channels make this very, very easy.

Learning New Skills

I love to learn new things, even if I never plan to do them myself. The better I understand how things work, the more prepared I can be with the right input, reducing the effort someone else must put into it to give me the output I want. Usually, less effort equates to lower costs too.

When I hired my first author services aggregator, they assigned me an interior-designer-slash-formatter. This person's purpose was to take the manuscript in its final form (after editing, proofing, etc.) and put it in two formats. The first (and easier) was a flowable (ebook) file.

I received the proof of the first ebook, and of course, being me, I asked questions. What could I have done differently to make the conversion easier? I learned about hidden codes in my word processing program and how to avoid using them, because they created conversion problems. My second book had none of those problems, but I hadn't put in the correct kinds of page breaks. I stowed away another valuable lesson.

> **Learn as little or as much as you care about – you don't need to learn it all right away.**

The second version of my file was the paperback proof. That had its own issues for conversion, with a few repeats. The layout became important, and I hadn't formatted my text to make that easy. Page breaks created some issues. Style codes created another. What was in the front matter and what in the back? Again, I learned new tricks.

I extended my learning process to cover design, where I saved the questionnaire the designer sent me. What did a designer consider important in representing a book? What were the tricks of making thumbnails, those mini versions of your book's cover, stand out on a book selling website? What went where on the cover and why?

My point to you is that you can learn as little or as much as you desire, as you have time for, and as you care about. I want to know as much as I can, because I want to be able to rely on me, myself and I to accomplish things. If I'm doing it, I don't have to wait to be fit into someone else's schedule. Things become faster and more flexible.

Am I the best at all tasks? No! I regularly send things out for a review of what I'm doing or how I'm doing it to learn from the suggestions. The first couple of books in a new series require more input than the tenth.

Your Three-Legged Stool

If you have the money and you'd rather spend your time writing, hire out as much as you can. If you have the skills and the money, ditto. If you have the skills but no money, learn to do things yourself. You can do it!

In this business, like any other, you get what you pay for. The cheapest is not always the best, though some people growing their reputation are amazing and fantastic and will accept lower compensation. Ask for references and talk to them. Check out the person's previous work if you can.

Buy wisely, because it's not only your money, but your indie reputation and brand being sent out into the reader universe. Remember, oversight is up to you. Don't rely on someone else to have your best self-publishing interests first in their minds. It's your indie brand. Guard it selfishly!

5 – OWN YOUR ISBNs

Almost any book site offers you the option of using one of their ISBNs when you upload through them, and some sites also offer you the option of uploading without an ISBN altogether. You don't always NEED an ISBN, but you should own them when you do use them.

ISBN stands for International Standard Book Number. Each country offering publishing registrations has a company designated as the repository of ISBNs in that country. When a book conversion or distribution site offers you a number, it comes out of the long list of numbers they've bought from the registration agency. They own that number – and they are happy to let you use it for a price.

Note that I said, 'let you use it'. You do not own it unless you buy it yourself. When you own that number, you become the publisher for that book. CONTROL. (You knew that was coming, right?)

In the U.S., our ISBN agency is a company called Bowker (www.isbn.org). They sell unique numbers to the big publishing houses, author services companies, and YOU. Everyone who needs a number in the U.S. buys it from them.

Following the Money, Part One

When you own your ISBN, you are the publisher of record. You can do WHATEVER you want with that title. Offer it on other distribution channels. Change the front or back matter or the cover. Take it down. You OWN it.

Some indie authors don't like to buy their own numbers because of the expense. I understand that it seems like a major investment. Anything that equals the check at a very nice dinner for two with wine feels like that, particularly when an author services company lets you have it for $20. It's time to think past that:

If you are only releasing one book through one distribution channel, use whatever they offer you. That will be your most cost-effective option.

If you plan to publish a string of books, buy a package from Bowker. Buy a bigger package than you think you'll need, as much as you can afford for your writing life.

I originally bought ISBNs from the author services company I worked with. When I wanted to take over control of the titles from that company to change distribution, I needed new ISBNs to do it. They owned the ones they 'gave' me. I then had to reissue the titles with my own ISBNs. Otherwise, the payment of royalties would continue to go to the author services company, who would take their cut and give me the (pitiful) remainder.

It's about following the money, people!

Let's review. *Whoever owns the ISBN gets the money FIRST*. That owner then decides, based on contract, how much goes to the author. (Wouldn't you rather have all of it go directly into your pocket? I thought so.)

How Many ISBNs

How many ISBNs do you need? More than you think. I'll use my book list as an example.

I originally bought a 10 pack. Where a single ISBN is that nice dinner, the price of 10 is a car payment for an average new vehicle. BUT – where (as of the time I'm typing this) a single ISBN costs $125, one number out of the 10 costs $29.50. And a 100 pack? That price drops to $5.75 a piece!

My 10-pack was gone before I knew it. I had four titles to transfer to my own control, and I already had two more books underway. Hhmmm. I bought a 100 pack on the next round, and for the record, I'm halfway through using it up too.

Where do the numbers go?

You need an ISBN for each format of the book.

That means ebook, paperback, and

hardback.

One title in ereader and paperback format

means at least two ISBN numbers.

On physical formats, you need one for each size

of the book too.

You can see how easy it is to run through them like water! Box set? Another ISBN, even though each title in the set has a number. Special edition for a specific distributor? Another ISBN. Paperback in mass market size to add to trade? Another. Yikes!

Sign up to receive emails from Bowker. They regularly run specials. Buy what you think you will need when things are on sale. It is easy to upload to their system, and your book is registered in the national database, giving you some leverage if someone tries to hijack the content of your book.

Barcodes

Barcodes are based on ISBNs, but they are not the same thing. For each physical version of your book that you plan to sell through any retail site, you need a barcode to put on the back cover. That's how retailers scan the book, and it's how you put the price on the book for that retailer.

Bowker sells you the barcodes too. You buy them singly or in a pack, and when you assign a title to an ISBN, you have the option to generate a barcode for that ISBN. It includes the price in the barcode, so you'll want to decide on your price first.

I bought barcodes singly in the beginning. There is no price break on them in quantity as there are for ISBNs. I finally got smart and bought them in packs when Bowker had a sale. Like my ISBNs, those barcodes belong to me as my own publishing company.

Copyright

People will tell you that your work is copyrighted as soon as you write it, which is true, if you can prove when you wrote it. No one can copy your work and claim it as their own without providing a citation attributing the work to you (and paying you for it if they profit from it without your permission).

Your book should have a copyright page in it. Go to traditionally published books in your genre and see how they structure this page, and use the style and features that make sense to you.

"But really, isn't that enough?" Here's reality. Are you really going to sue someone for taking your book? How will you prove it? Can you afford it? No on any or all counts? File a copyright. Putting that certificate number on your copyright page may dissuade evil-doers.

There are providers who will offer to help you file your copyright for a fee. You don't need to pay anyone else to do it, unless you're completely technology adverse.

AS SOON AS YOUR BOOK IS IN FINAL, FINAL, FINAL FORM, *do it yourself.* Go to the U.S. Copyright Office online (www.copyright.gov). You set up an account, and you enter the information about your title. You pay a fee, which you would also have to pay if you pay someone else to do this for you. The application is easy to complete. If your book is only in ebook format, you send them the file. If it is also in paper, I've found it's better to send them the requisite two copies. Why it makes a difference is something that's a mystery with the agency behind the curtain.

In about two months, maybe three, you receive a nice certificate in the mail. That's your copyright. You put that number on the copyright page when you next update your book on whatever sites you use to distribute it.

By the way, Bowker also offers a paid copyrighting module. They bundle that with ISBNs and barcodes for a discount on each part individually, and sometimes, the bundle goes on sale too. If you'd rather not be bothered filing with the Feds yourself, this might be a good choice for you. It's another way of keeping more dollars in your pocket as an indie publishing house.

Keeping Your Control

Recapping this section, I can't reiterate frequently enough how important owning your ISBN is for your control of your indie business. The barcode is a necessity, a required business expense. The copyright protects your right, one you already have but, let's face it, someone might try to steal. But the ISBN? That's the money, baby!

6 – DEMAND ACCOUNTABILITY

Now that we've had the ISBN discussion, I can move on to those who want to use an author services company anyway. (The good ones will let you assign your own ISBN from those you own – just sayin'.) Even if you can maintain ISBN control, there are other areas where practicing business caution is a necessity.

I'm talking about accountability, the confidence that you can trust the reporting you receive on your sales and track the dollars rolling to you from royalties.

Following the Money, Part Two

Money is king. Accountability is queen, and she's hanging out with her consort, transparency.

Many good reasons might drive you to owning your ISBN and uploading your book directly to the sites you use to distribute it. Even in cases where someone else gives you the

ISBN, or when you use a service provider to do the uploading for you, you should be careful about the money part.

Accountability is the type of nitpicking you might expect from auditors. (I was one once.) Transparency sides on the management consulting side of my personality. For your purposes, accountability is what your business partners should be able to do to track the money flowing through their coffers and into yours. Transparency is their willingness and ability to share that trail with YOU.

You'll fall under one of three broad money models:

> *You own your ISBN and you upload the book directly to the distributor. They pay your royalty directly to you on their schedule, usually two months after the sale.*
> *You own your ISBN and you use a service to do the uploading. The distributor pays the service two months later. The service aggregates your royalties and pays on their schedule – usually monthly.*

You use the ISBN provided to you by the service
doing the uploading. The distributor pays
the service two months later. The service
aggregates your royalties and pays on
their schedule – like every six months for
the previous six-month period.

Yes, these are models in between, but these are the most common. Know the terms and conditions of yours and get it in writing.

In ANY of these cases, you want accountability. What books were sold? What geographic market? What retail price? Most importantly, can you reconcile the royalties you received with the deposit?

Yes, accountability is a hot button for me, because I still don't know what I was paid for in that first year, when I worked with an author services company. I don't know which titles sold. I don't know what distribution channel they sold on. I don't know how much people paid to buy the book after discounts and I didn't have access to the calculation behind my royalty payment. I trusted that this was the way the industry worked (which reminded me of the era of abacuses) and relied on the similar experiences of others who shared my same issues. Don't make my mistake!

Most direct distribution channels have strong dashboards for sales reporting. You can see the number of units you sold, and often can even tell what country they sold in if you are the publisher of record (ISBN owner). Price and discounts are revealed, as are any fees for downloading, delivery, printing and shipping. Your royalty calculation is clear, meaning you understand how the retail amount paid trickled through the system to become the bucks in your bank account.

This detailed information, though, is too often lost when it disappears behind the curtain of a services company. Not all companies are like this – and I will say I've worked with some who were great too. Be wary and ask questions. You want to see an example of the kind of reporting you can access on demand. Almost everyone pays royalties on direct deposit when it accumulates to a specific dollar amount. You want to see the units you sold to support that balance.

Ask how quickly their records of sales are updated. If, for example, you're running a promotional campaign, you want to know if it's having an impact. Are people buying the title you're promoting? If you're spending your hard-earned money for advertising, you want to know if it's working – or not.

Get It in Writing

I have a management consulting background. I cut my eyeteeth on agreements codifying the work to be performed, performance schedules, and deliverables. I never charged an hour of billable time without a contract.

And *despite* this, I still allowed myself to be rolled over when it came time to hire a company to help me finalize and distribute my books. "This is the way we do things," they'd say. Or, "It's all on our website." Or, my fav, "Trust me."

Ah, no.

> **Being an indie author means being a**
>
> **BUSINESS.**

If you are an indie author, you are a BUSINESS. You are the CEO, file clerk, and director of creative ideas. You are the penultimate EVERYBODY. Even when you hire people, you are still IN CHARGE.

I find that professionals in the publishing field often already have standard agreements they want you to sign. That's good, great, even, as long as you read them, question anything you don't understand, and negotiate the things you don't agree with. There is no harm in asking for something different. If they say no and it's a deal breaker for you, both parties walk away with no hard feelings.

It's much worse to end up with bad feelings between you (and less than stellar work and support) because someone didn't like a condition of the contract but didn't speak up. Or someone misses a major deadline, delaying the release. And worst case, you end up in court. <<SHIVERS>>

Who Else Do I Need?

The usual suspects for a writing project come to mind, but think as well about the support personnel, the ones who work behind the scenes to make your writing life more productive. Here's a representative list of the types of professionals I consider vital to build a viable indie publishing house:

Editor ***

Proofreader ***

Formatter ***

Cover designer ***

Website designer

Virtual (or live) assistant

Accountant

Intellectual property attorney

Estate/family law attorney

Publicist

That's just the beginning. You could throw in housekeeping, gardening, child care, and any other repetitive task that pulls you away from your indie writing life. Focus your energy on CEO/writerly activities, and leave the rest to someone who is a professional in that field. (That being said, it is time for me to fold laundry.)

I Can't Afford This!

Yes, you can. You can't afford NOT to hire them. You don't need all of them at once, but eventually, because you are going to be *successful* at this author thing, you will need them all.

If I could only afford part of this list, I'd begin with the four starred roles above. If you cannot afford them, try trading services. Are you already good at cover art? Find someone who can edit your work in exchange for a book cover. You love formatting, but website design, not so much. Trade services! Be creative in this as well as your writing work, because ignoring one of these vital steps might result in a lower quality product – and that will send your readers running away faster than an Olympic-grade sprinter.

7 – DOCUMENT YOUR METADATA

You will forget, along around book three or four, where you have distributed your series to date and how you have your identification set up. I'm talking metadata, the holy grail of book information. What version or edition? When did you upload it? What are the price points? What promotions have you run?

Metadata and the other miscellanea about your books build an important database for readers to find you, and for you to connect with your readers. Let's say, for example, that you use a free magnet link in your books. (A magnet is a free book you give away to readers in exchange for them giving you their email addresses and permission to send them messages, to build your mailing list.) I had a free magnet, but I wasn't happy with it. I didn't believe it adequately represented my writing style or the series.

The link to the magnet appeared at the front and back of each ebook. Not only was the cover included but a blurb about the book was meant to attract a reader to share their contact info with me. Changing the magnet required a change to the non-story interior for each ebook. That meant uploading fresh versions of each title to each site, with the link to the new book. If you have three titles available on only one distribution site, it might not be such a big deal. Ten times five? Yikes!

> **The devil and all his minions are in the details. It pays to keep track of them.**

Or, you decide your book blurb, its vital description used to lure readers to buy, is a clear miss. You have a new, targeted, tremendous version – but where do you need to replace the worn out one? The same goes for better keywords and genre categories. Any information available about that title might need to be updated when you make a course correction on how you represent the book or the series.

Metadata Recordkeeping

Maintaining good records of what is where can take any form you like – a text list, a spreadsheet, an index card, or a wing and a prayer in your gray matter. I like things written down, so I don't have to clog up the synapses remembering. I use a combination of text files and spreadsheets.

For each title, I have a text file called 'description – (book title)'. It contains:

Book title, subtitle

Book tagline

Hero, heroine

Book description – long version and short version

Description without and with HTML codes for bold and italics formatting

Advertising taglines and texts

Keywords, by distribution channel

Genre categories, by distribution channel

BISAC codes, by distribution channel

A little background will help you understand why I use all of this. Some sites want a long description, and in some places, you're limited to 100 words. You will be able to cut and paste a formatted description, including bold and italics, into some sites, and some will not accept anything other than plain text unless you use HTML codes.

The number of keywords you're allowed on each site varies. Your choices of genre category differ. Book Industry Standards and Communications (BISAC) codes are subject classifications established by the Book Industry Study Group (BISG). These are widely used by libraries, wholesale distributors, and other marketers to examine the books in a genre category. Some sites let you use one, and some, three.

My design of this text file evolved over the years. I now have major headings I use each time, and sometimes, if, for example, I have a string of book reviews I want to highlight, it might contain additional sections. The list I'm giving you is what I would consider a minimum.

Numbers in One Place

Now to the numeric part, where I use a spreadsheet. There is no specific *reason* I use a spreadsheet program instead of more text, except that I like spreadsheets.

Down the left side of the spreadsheet, I have each title listed. When I say each title, I mean EACH. That means if I have the same book but had to release different versions for different distribution channels (different ISBNs is how I classify 'different'), a title might be listed multiple times. Ditto for different paperback format sizes.

The column headings are:

Book title/version

My shorthand number for it

Release date

Ebook ISBN

Paperback ISBN

Library of Congress Copyright number

Ebook price

Paperback price

A column for each distribution channel

Whew! Having the grid of what's where all available in one place is the reason I use a spreadsheet. Right now, I put an X in the box if a title is distributed in that channel, but I could see a need to put the price I use in that box instead, in case I had to vary pricing. I have 24 columns with distribution channels at this point.

Before you ask, yes, this could ALL be on a text file. Likewise, ALL of this could be in a database instead of two distinct places. Someday, if I'm really bored and want to play with my laptop, I might build that database.

I'd rather write new words. How about you?

Leaving a Trail

None of us like to think about this, but someday, we won't be walking this planet. Someday, someone coming behind us will ask, "Where are her books? Where are his royalties coming from? What does the estate own? Who owns the rest?"

They'll be looking for this file, so tell your legal executor or the person in charge of future financial activities where it is. It's part of your legacy, and what you leave behind keeps earning an income like any investment. Treat the recordkeeping for it as such.

8 – AVOID TECHNOLOGY DISTRACTIONS

I use a mix of software programs and low-tech solutions to manage my author business, and you will too. There is no single best way – only the way YOU WILL USE AND KEEP UPDATED that's best. What I mention here is *in no way* an endorsement, other than I use them and found them to be helpful *to me*. You might not like them. I think I've satisfied the legal department now.

There is no single solution for all author needs. I wish there was! A slew of tools, though, can make your author life easier. For example, I use Scrivener to convert my books from Microsoft Word format to MOBI and EPUB for books I plan to give away myself. But I didn't always do it this way, because the learning curve for Scrivener is steep, and I didn't feel like I had the time to master it. I therefore bypassed opportunities that required converted files.

Along similar lines, I experimented with most of the social media platforms out there until I settled on the ones that worked for me. I use Hootsuite to schedule posts across the sites I'm active on, and/or I post directly one by one, depending on what I'm posting and how much patience I have. But Hootsuite wasn't always in my repertoire and my time couldn't always be spent on multiple postings, so I wasn't always as active as I could have been.

WORD COUNT COMES FIRST

I can't emphasize this enough. WORD COUNT COMES FIRST. A team of people could have a full-time job learning all available tools for writers, implementing said tools, and managing the uploads and postings for them. Unless you have a staff of assistants, you'll have to spend your time wisely.

Repeat after me. "WORD COUNT COMES FIRST."

If you have a day job and commute, busy family life, or loads of other obligations, the time you spend on your author life might be limited. Don't spend it fiddling with technology until you've written your goal of new words for the day, or edited to the point you've set for yourself. None of that support technology will mean ANYTHING unless you have a solid manuscript to sell.

My schedule changes from day to day. I wish it was static, like I wrote every day from 7 in the morning for three hours, and then could get on with my day. My life isn't like that. Some things must be done first thing in the morning. Some out of office (which means out of our house) tasks can't easily be switched to another time without incurring significant cost or hardship.

Besides, I find that I'm not the kind of person who likes a routine. Other than the rule that **I WRITE DAILY**, the exact word count or project is dynamic. On some days, I write 5,000 words in two hours. On others, I might be editing and feel lucky to make it through a chapter in three hours. It just depends.

WORDS FIRST – Technology Later

The point is, I show up for as long as I can, until I've run the well dry and then some. I use Microsoft Word instead of pen and paper because my handwriting is atrocious (sorry, Sister Mary Alice).

AND THEN... I learn a new trick on software, or I try a new database, or I explore a new distribution channel. It comes AFTER the work of words. (And frankly, it's often harder, too! The writing and editing are the fun parts.)

One Place You Shouldn't Scrimp

Your manuscripts are like raw diamonds. They can be cut and polished for lucrative earning potential. Don't lose your diamonds because you have holes in your pockets.

This is one place where you should not scrimp, and that's managing your versions and formats. Imagine for a moment the simple ebook. You prepare it for distribution by adding a list of your titles in the front or back. Your readers LOVE this book and want to buy all the rest. To make it uber-easy for them, each title on that list is a live link to buy that book.

That sounds simple enough – except you are uploading this version to Distributor A. The ebook links need to drive the reader to buy on Distributor A's channel. You now have a version specific to A, but not B.

You can see where I'm going with this. Whatever naming convention you use for the electronic files in your computer, make sure it indicates whose version it is.

I will mention one other snafu that makes version control important. It's always a good idea to invite reviews of your book. If you happen to mention a mega-distributor in that call to action, and this version of your book is being distributed through another major channel, they might refuse to upload your book because it mentions a rival.

How can you keep a good trail of which version goes where? I use a naming convention that includes the following:

Title of the book

Ebook/distributor this version belongs on

File format (like DOC or PDF or EPUB)

Year of the release (or even date)

My formats end up looking something like: **Title Year Channel Format**, with a space between each word. The files for each book live in a unique electronic file folder. Each series contains the file folders of all its books. Find a cataloging method that works for the way you think, and stick to it! (Don't forget to back-up often too!)

Social Media, Blogging and Other Hubbub

Many discussions swirl around social media for authors these days. Which channels should you use? How frequently should you post to them? What should you offer? Can you ask them to buy your book? Is a newsletter required? What about a blog?

The answers are:

> *Use the channels your readers use. AND use the channels that work for you in terms of time and effort.*
>
> *Post as frequently as you have something meaningful to say that will be important TO THEM.*

Offer things about your inspirations, progress, writing life, or themes that make you more approachable TO THEM.

Ask them to buy your book, but DON'T make that the only thing you ever send them.

Writing a newsletter is your choice – but only if you have something you want to tell them that doesn't fit in your other messaging methods. It takes time to produce well, time you might better spend writing your next book.

Ditto on the blog.

Yes, this section is important to any author's interactions with their readers. Trad, hybrid or indie, unless you can afford to hire a publicist yourself, you'll be doing this – yourself. And readers love that!

The public persona you post to the world at large is just that – public. It isn't about you. Readers want to feel like they become familiar with YOU through the posts, newsletters, and pictures you feature. It is all about THEM.

Learn Your Audience

Granted, it can be hard to figure out who buys your books. Your potential audience is largely blocked from your direct view, unless you have direct contact with them through your presence. Can you imagine a handful of your readers, by age, gender, ethnicity, life goals, life experiences? Where would they hang out?

I've used various methods to figure out who my readers are, and where they spend their free time online. The one I've found most effective is getting to know them well when I do meet them somehow. This happens face to face at book events, through responses to enewsletters or blog posts, and through the statistics I mine like a crusty old prospector whenever I run an ad. I make assumptions from the people I meet face to face or virtually about my audience as a whole.

> **Value your readers by avoiding the constant beg-a-thon. Treat them as well as you'd treat your best friends.**

The other way to learn more about your crowd is to ask them for feedback. Surveys are terrific for learning what makes your readers tick, how they find you, and how they find their next book to read. If you engage via survey, make sure there's something in it for them. Many quick virtual survey tools exist, and many of them are free for limited numbers of questions or respondents.

Open-ended questions, the kind that can't only be answered with a check on a list or yes/no, are great for teasing out more detailed information. They also drive some people crazy. Checklists are terrific for narrowing down options and telling people what you're really interested in knowing. Some of your audience will hate those too, so the best bet is a combination of the two styles.

Be careful about what you ask, though. Make sure that if their responses indicate an action you should be taking, you *want* to take that action. For example, if you ask what social media channels they frequent, but social media isn't for you, it's a wasted effort (other than to tell you a change in your own thinking may be required). If you ask them how often they like to hear from their favorite authors, and they tell you quarterly, you have something actionable to decide upon as a result.

Email List Control

You've undoubtedly heard this before, because it can't be emphasized enough. Own your email list! You might have 10,000 followers on a social media site – and then that site changes the rules of engagement. A core group of a few hundred on another are great for a street team of people who build buzz about your book, but if you can't send them something directly because it's against the host company's rules, that list is less useful.

Workshops, classes, and consultancies have been built the how-to's of building a list you own. I've taken some of them, agree with some of their premises, and have had luck with my own list. But the facts of the matter can make this very simple:

Every time you interact with a new potential

reader, make the engagement

memorable for THEM. Then ask for their

email address.

Every time a fan of yours expresses their

appreciation, ask them for suggestions

on how you can reach more people like

them, who might enjoy your work.

Begin gathering email addresses well before you

have anything to sell them. This isn't

about selling. It's about ENGAGEMENT.

Honestly, fans are much smarter about our work than we are, because they can see it more clearly. They didn't give birth to the characters, the plot, the conflict, the happy ending. We, as creatives, are personally invested in our products. Our fans are the ones enjoying them.

Once you have something to say, send something out to your email list. Many writers send out free sections of upcoming books. Others send out background information, like a travelogue about a place they visited for research. They sponsor giveaways or have contests, both painless with today's technology tools. Still others reveal things about their non-writing passions, as I do about travel and places I visit.

Bottom line – reach out to readers as you would like to be contacted, with the kind of information that isn't pushy, buy-buy-buy, or a waste of their time. They will unsubscribe, and it will be ten times harder to win them back again. Plus, they'll tell their friends to avoid your list!

People will subscribe no matter what. I do, on a regular basis, from almost every e-list I'm on. Then I decide what I miss, and I may subscribe again to those. It's not unusual to have up to ten percent of your list unsubscribe each time you send out something, up to the time when you are down to a core group of people who are truly interested in your work and YOU. (And then you'll still lose some.)

While you have a plan to hold on to your subscribers through great engagement, you also need a plan to gather new ones to replace those who leave you. I earn permission to turn an interested person into a subscriber through:

Sign-up sheets at events

'Follow me' buttons on social media

Newsletter sign-up form on my website

Free books people can download when they

share their email

Contests, promotions and giveaways where

people earn free books in exchange for

their email

Those final two are the least likely to result in a true follower. Face it, people *like* free. If you have enough books in a series or something else representative of your work and you believe in the power of free, use it. Some of these folks will leave you as soon as they have the freebie. That's okay. If they like what they see, they'll buy more. If they don't, you don't have a platform to sell them anyway.

Technology as a Tool

Like everything else in your writer's arsenal, technology is a tool. Not everyone needs to use it in the same way. You can write with a quill pen, ink well and scroll paper. (That makes self-publishing a tad more challenging, but you can work with it!) Find the tools that fit best in YOUR hands and focus on those. As time allows, after you've written yourself to a stopping point, consider what else you might want to try to expand your capabilities and reach.

9 – PROMOTE THYSELF

We would all LOVE to experience it. Your name and face, splashed across a half-page ad in a major magazine or featured as the bottom runner in a newspaper with significant circulation, means the clerk at the grocery store and the people in line recognize you. Your book, featured on a talk show personality's must-read list, interviewed by said personality, with off-the-charts spikes in sales, brings review recognition. Your favorite big-name author, the one you fangirl/fanguy about, posts a link to your book on social media because they adore what you wrote.

> **PROMOTION is YOUR job.**

Basically, we want someone to draw attention to our excellent work, because doing it ourselves is *hard*. Most writers are introverts. We ponder, ruminate, and analyze. We seek perfection. We want someone to like us, really, *really* like us. It's difficult not to take the attention, or lack thereof, personally. If they don't like our book, something must be wrong with US. That makes it harder to do self-promotion.

Promotion = Our Responsibility

Whether you are indie or trad or hybrid, promotion will be on YOUR to-do list. Traditional publishers often lack the budget and the bandwidth to run a campaign to tell the world about how terrific YOUR book is, especially if you are a new author. They barely have the budget for big name folks. Don't take it personally.

What you SHOULD take personally is how much you can do to promote yourself.

I mentioned social media before, and I mentioned branding. Those are avenues within your overall outreach strategy. And you do need a strategy. It can be as big or as little as you feel you can cope with. Whatever you do, it should be a plan that begins long before you release your book. Or begin as soon as you can, if you're close to release already. Or begin NOW if you already have books out there, and you've done little, hoping they will (magically) find their audience.

Easy Outreach

You might think I'm going to list the many ways you can use social media ads or newsletters or giveaways. I'm not. I'm going to talk about how YOU put yourself out there and shout to the world **I AM A WRITER**. (And buy my books, but that's secondary.)

The title of this section can be misleading. Yes, it is deceptively simple in terms of the WHAT part. It will be hard for many of us – scratch that, most of us – to do. We must tell the world who we are and own our work, in PUBLIC.

Here's an example of this in action from my day. On errands day, dear hubby and I hit the major stops – the ubiquitous coffee chain with the green mermaid cups, the post office, the bank, the chain household goods retailer, the grocery store. We've lived in this area for a while now, and we know a lot of people at a lot of places. I'm the writer, the OUTGOING writer.

Remember when I talked about writers tending to be introverts? I am at the *extreme* introvert end of that spectrum! I was so shy as a child that our neighbor in Chicago used to give me a quarter as a reward for coming out from behind my dad. As a teenager, I took a job at a women's clothing store for minimum wage plus commissions, using money as a motivator to channel a bubbly sales personality that wasn't native to my psyche.

I've been a management consultant for decades, which means talking to many different people on any given project. I had my own practice for twenty years, and the responsibility for sales and marketing fell on my shoulders. No clients, no business, no paycheck. As a university professor, I spoke in front of students in groups large and small, and I spoke on professional topics with hundreds in an audience.

I taught myself to be an extrovert.

Trained Extrovert Made Simple

I'm not saying this is easy, but it is do-able. Better yet, I should say that if I can do it, anyone can! I trained myself to "be" with people, like playing a role in an imaginary movie. I don't do it every day, and I don't do it in every situation, but I make it count when I do.

Back to errands day. I know most of the people working at this well-known coffee chain store, because we go in every week a couple of times and I talk them up. You might have caught that. *I talk them up.* I make a point of learning their names, and greeting them with a smile, a comment they'll remember, or a self-directed joke. As a result, they remember me.

When someone new comes on board, they don't know me yet, but the others do, and relationships are viral. When everyone lights up the minute you come in, everyone who doesn't know you wants part of that action. We're human. We crave society and relationship, even when we're introverts.

On this particular day, the barista is a person I haven't talked to before. She asked, as they are trained to do, what we have going on today. I said, "Errands, then back to work." "Oh, sorry about the work part," she replied.

Enter the trained extrovert with her spiel. "I'm a writer," I said, "so it's fun. I love creating stories."

I have learned that one of three things happen when you introduce yourself as a writer:

> *They're inside their heads and aren't paying attention to anything other than counting down the hours left in their day and what's inside they're head. They can't hear you. MOVE ON.*
>
> *They aren't readers, so the fact that you're a writer doesn't matter to them. But they do SOMETHING with their free time. LEARN MORE.*
>
> *They love to read (because it seems like people either don't do it or love it) and they want to know if you've published anything. CUE THE BUSINESS CARDS.*

Remember, in any of these scenarios, your job as a trained extrovert is to BUILD A RELATIONSHIP with them. Even if they never buy your book, you want them to talk about you being a writer in public, so people who do buy books overhear it. The simple act of making eye contact and actively listening to someone lets them know they MATTER.

I pay close attention to human behavior. In the first scenario, the care-less case, that person could be having a bad day. I can lift them up, and I bring a smile to their face by recognizing they need a lift. People remember the kindness and the empathy (not sympathy, but empathy). They remember YOU. They might talk to you when they talk to no one else, not about heavy things, but recognizing you.

Relationship of a different kind builds from the second scenario. A checker at the grocery store isn't a big reader, but his mother wrote a memoir she now wants to self-publish. I offered to help her out with advice when she's ready, which he really appreciated. I ask about her book each time I see him, because I am truly interested in seeing her succeed. That cued the business cards exchange, which I'll get to in a minute.

Moving on to the third scenario, the avid reader, it's easy to see how this turns into a potential reader, follower and sale. They read, and you are an author. It doesn't matter what genre, most of the time. Readers love to meet authors. They want to know you better, and you want to develop a relationship with them, even if they don't read your kind of books. (Someday, you might write what they like, or someone they know already likes your genre.) Send them to wherever they can find you.

As a twist on the third scenario, someone might have suggestions for you that make sense. Waiting at the fish counter, we ran into our physician. (Good thing it was the fish counter, and not a packaged foods aisle!) She hadn't seen us all summer (which was a good thing, I thought) and wanted to know what we'd been up to. We told her about a road trip, which led to a discussion about how much she loves road trips too, and I told her a fast story about my love of road trips stemming from adventurous childhood travels.

"You should write about that," she said. "I blogged about it," I replied. She didn't know I had a blog. She wanted to know more about it – and our relationship was taken to another level. She might not read my books, but she'll read my blogs, which are, by and large, personal stories.

Cue the Business Cards

I am never without my business cards. ALMOST NEVER EVER. They are an inexpensive form of relationship building, and the least costly method of print advertising you will find.

When someone wants to know about what I write, I give them cards. Not one, but two or three. I say something like, "Please, take a couple, and share them with your friends." Yes, some might end up tossed. I won't know, and I'm not hurt by the idea. Hand them out freely to anyone who might express an interest.

I gave them to the grocery checker to share with his mom. She belongs to a writers group, I learned during our discussions, so I gave him a stack. She could share them with her group too. I could be a resource to anyone who wants to know more about self-publishing.

Writers are readers too. Just sayin'...

My doctor has my cards to find my website and my blog. She has people in her office who love to read. "Here, take a few more." Bonus points mount up when others in your vicinity overhear her. I once had a woman walk up to me as I left the grocery store because she heard me discussing my current writing project with my favorite reader/checker, and she wanted a know more!

You might note I said 'almost' about being without my cards. I was recently in Belize on vacation, heading for a day of snorkeling. I didn't have my wallet, so, no cards. (Really, they'd get wet anyway!) The clerk at the dive shop counter was a reader, though. She asked if I was on a book review site she prefers. When I said yes, she whipped out her phone and plugged in my name – and put one of my titles on her must-read list. If you are caught without cards, ask if the person has access to a book listing site and find yourself there instead.

What if you aren't yet published? That's ok. *You want to build the relationships NOW.* Make them interested in your work. They might read you someday when your book is out there, AND they'll ask you about it. On a day when you think it's not worth it, you don't have a reason to write anymore, their question might be the thing you need to put your fingers back on the keyboard.

DON'T Do This If You're Not 'On'

There are days when I don't want to talk to anyone. I don't want to be noticed. I could care less about relationships! But I should go out in public for some reason.

Don't try to be a trained extrovert if you're not ready to be 'on'. The results will not be pretty. You might jeopardize a potential relationship because someone feels snubbed. You'll become the snotty writer in their mind. Will they then want to read your book? No!

How can you deal with this? Create a boundary or a barrier. A boundary limits your interactions. A barrier locks them.

I've used earbuds or headphones as a boundary. I might point at the headset and phone and mouth 'conference call', and people understand and nod and don't feel like they weren't important to me. Sympathetic glances might be exchanged. I blend into the surroundings and stare at the face of my phone or put a hand to my ear. My interaction with them is limited by the situation I'm in.

Barriers, on the other hand, don't give people an opportunity to engage at all. The one I employ most frequently here is a lack of eye contact. Keeping your eyes on a laptop screen or a list or a phone means engagement with others is impossible. Unless, of course, they force the issue. If you need a better guarantee that won't happen, employ the headphones along with the lack of eye contact.

Little Bites, Little Wins

This is what you're after. Little ways reach people who can matter in your writer life. When all else fails, wear a t-shirt in public that proclaims you are a writer and invites people to ask you about what you write. You don't need to take giant steps when little bites will do, and they might mean more for you in the long run. Building relationships with your audience helps you learn more about what appeals to them, and that can help inform your writing, your outreach, and your success.

10 – BUILD YOUR WRITING TRIBE

Humans are social creatures, even as introverts. We crave contact with others who understand our feelings and ambitions. Tribes didn't go out with the cave dwellers era. Today, as disconnected as we are in so many realms, we need our personal tribe even more.

Networking Breeds Success

Networking means finding others who speak our language and interacting with them. We can't learn it all alone. We can't see our shortcomings without a mirror held by those who can be honest about our work. We won't get far if the only voice we're hearing is our own. We need to network.

Networking can take many forms, and each of those can lead to building a tribe. I belong to multiple tribes because each feed a different writing need of mine. I found my tribes through several resources:

Writers organization (formal)

Writers group (informal)

Virtual online loops (formal and informal)

Collaborative of creatives (masterminds)

Conferences and workshops

Service providers

That's just the beginning. It's not always easy for an introvert to be a joiner, but it gets easier each time I do it.

How I Built My Tribe

When I decided to write fiction full time, I existed in that happy place where I didn't know stuff. Lots of stuff. Major stuff. But I was willing to learn.

I studied, researched, and surfed. I read magazines about writing, and took online courses. I wrote like a fiend, and I studied my work against these resources. That wasn't enough, though, because the only voice I heard was my own.

I had to take a BIG STEP. I had to J-O-I-N something. I had to own my identity as a newbie fiction writer, even when that meant I had to expose my naivete. I was convinced everyone in whatever writing room I entered was going to be someone who got it – all of it – and sold lots of books.

> **I would be lost without my writing tribe.**

That didn't dissuade me. I found a national organization in my genre, and I learned about their local chapter. I signed up, and I showed up. My world tilted in a very excellent way.

Not only did that group provide me with training on topics I needed, but it also brought me the members of my first writing tribe. The larger circle of authors in this chapter embraced me, guided me, and supported me. They understood what I was going through. Their advice, built on accumulated years of knowledge and experience, served me well.

My small tribe of tight-knit friends within this larger group are with me still. Back in those original days, only one of us was published. Today, only one isn't, and that's because her demanding day job and family life make it hard for her to write and edit as fast as she'd like. We prop each other up when one of us wants to quit. We scream with joy about each person's success. We celebrate the wins and mourn the losses and strategize about how to make our work better.

If I hadn't joined that formal national structure, I would never have met these amazing writers and authors. They led me to other resources. I attend conferences and workshops where I continue to evolve in my craft. I teach what I know, giving back and strengthening the tribe overall. Through them I've found virtual organizations specializing in aspects unique to my style of writing. I added local face-to-face writers' groups to the mix, from different genres but sharing the love of writing in common.

I wanted to take things to a new level, so I moved outside the writing zone to other kinds of artists. I joined a creative collaborative, a virtual mastermind that focuses on how to be more creative and grow our businesses. Some are visual artists, some are photographers or podcasters, and some are writers in genres different from mine. They challenge me to think about my work in new ways. And again, they offer me an opportunity to give back. I learn from the teaching as well as the learning.

Introverts Hate Conferences

Three days, in public, interacting with people. It can be an introvert's worst nightmare. It can also be your best friend.

I would attend more conferences if I could afford it. It's not just the money, but the time. The energy of staying engaged with others while filling my head with ideas results in a need to hide in my cave for a week afterwards! I always feel like I should throw out everything I'm working on and start over, because what I learn feels overwhelming.

I go anyway. I talk to people. I make friends. I reach out. *I INVEST IN MY CRAFT.*

Here's how to make your conference experience better for your introverted self:

Pick a conference that will teach you craft or business skills.

Select a conference in your genre, offering training in things you want to know. You'll be more excited about attending.

Expect to be overwhelmed. We all are in those settings. It's the thrill of great ideas and people who UNDERSTAND US.

Stay in the conference hotel so you're in the middle of the action.

Carry your business cards everywhere, and share them liberally.

Write notes on the back of the ones you receive to remind you about that person.

Scared? Someone there is more frightened and shy than you. Find that person and invite them to be your buddy. You'll both be stronger for it.

Talk to people. No one bites. If they do, they aren't part of your tribe. Even the person who did that great lunchtime keynote speech is probably an introvert, like you.

LEARN! Take notes, even if you never look at them again. Things sink in through the acts of writing, listening, and observing. You'll learn more than you believe.

FOLLOW UP. It doesn't take long to send a brief email, reminding them how they know you and thanking someone for their time. That person may be say exactly what you need to hear when you next need to hear it the most.

It's okay to be geeky and fan-ish and out there at a conference. You're there to learn, to experience and to build friendships. You will be exhausted in all the best ways afterwards, and ready to tackle whatever your muse throws at you.

Writing Community Nonwriters

Nonwriters are part of the writing community too. Their primary focus is our service work. They get us. Outside of being their bread and butter, they understand how writers tick.

I mentioned already how much I learned from the service providers I hired. I ask them for feedback, for examples of things I could do better, for ways to make both our lives easier. I want recommendations, too, on who else they think might be a good match for me and my work.

In short, your writing tribe should be comprised of anyone who lifts you when you're down, improves the quality of your products, and supports your creative life. Seek out these people and hold on to them, tight. Put a hand out to the ones who come after you, and be willing to accept the wisdom of those ahead of you. That's what tribes do.

THE FINAL RULE

The final lesson is simple: **ALL RULES ARE MADE TO BE CHALLENGED.**

Wait, I just gave you ten suggestions, things many might consider rules. In reality, you can do whatever you want. Authors do it all the time. Some of them are BIG NAMES. The ones who aren't are not ones we hear about, in 99.99% of the cases.

You should do as much or as little as you can manage. Can't afford to pay someone to do it all and can't learn it yourself? Take more time to release your title and do what you can, when you can. Don't have time, but want to keep control? Write solid contracts with your service providers with realistic expectations and objective, quantifiable goals.

There is a solution for every problem – if you're willing to fight your innate resistance and accept it.

That is what all of this amounts to. Acceptance, for the way things are, for your piece of the process, for what your work will become. Yes, we'll all cross our fingers that your title is the next mega-bestseller.

We'll also celebrate your release by itself no matter what, because that's a BIG deal! It is said that over 80% of us would like to write a book. Very few of us do it, though, sticking with it through to THE END.

Releasing it via self-publishing? You've got this!

You've already done the hard part, writing the words!

Happy publishing, indies!

Also by Yvonne Kohano

GOOSE YOUR MUSE – TIPS FOR CREATIVES

Four Steps to Being a More Creative You

Four Steps to Business Planning for Plan-Phobic Creatives

10 Things I Wish I'd Known About Self-Publishing

MIND WEB PSYCHOLOGICAL THRILLER SERIES

Mind Stalked, Book 1

Mind Etched, Book 2

Mind Tangled, Book 3

FLYNN'S CROSSING ROMANTIC SUSPENSE SERIES

Pictures of Redemption, Book 1

Flashes of Fire, Book 2

Naked Intolerances, Book 3

Tastes and Consequences, Book 4

Blooms on the Bones, Book 5

Wine Into Water, Book 6

Love's Touch of Justice, Book 7

Measure Twice, Love Once, Book 8

Love's Fiery Prescription, Book 9

Love's Fiery Resolution, Book 10

Riffing with the Muse, Book 11

Flynn's Crossing Seasonal Novellas:

Three Blind Dates

Love and the Christmas Tree Nymph

This Proposal Between Us

Gratefully Ever Yours

State Fair Date Dare

Faded Family Photograph

And more to come!

Learn about upcoming releases at www.YvonneKohano.com.

About the Author

Award winning storycatcher Yvonne Kohano writes

contemporary romantic suspense, psychological thrillers, and

nonfiction tips on creativity, when she's not gardening, cooking,

traveling, reading or learning something new. Follow her at

www.YvonneKohano.com (psychological thriller and romantic

suspense fiction), and Facebook and Twitter to learn what

tickles her about being a writer.

Please leave an honest review of this nonfiction work at

your favorite book discovery site of choice. I love to hear from

readers, so feel free to contact me directly on Facebook as

Yvonne Kohano, on Twitter @yvonnekohano, and at

yvonne@yvonnekohano.com.

www.ingramcontent.com/pod-product-compliance
Lightning Source LLC
Chambersburg PA
CBHW061742020426
42331CB00006B/1330